THE OFFICIAL

Heart of Midlothian

ANNUAL 2018

Written by Sven Houston

Designed by Mathew Whittles

A Grange Publication

ISBN 978-1-911287-71-1

Contents

M.SMITH
2
Save the Children
16
27
umbro

The Captain

Hello and welcome to the Official Heart of Midlothian Football Club Annual 2018.

I had the pleasure of returning to this great football club ahead of the 2017/18 season and I must admit it feels great to be home again. Ever since I left Hearts back in 2009, I've always had it in the back of my head that I would one day come back to pull on the maroon jersey again. Needless to say, I jumped at the chance to return when the opportunity presented itself and I was honoured to be awarded the captain's armband.

Captaining Hearts is a tremendous privilege and something that I take very seriously. We have an incredible fan base that backs the club through thick and thin and it is my responsibility to help ensure every Hearts fan has a team they can be proud of.

The 2017/18 season is a big one for the club for a variety of reasons. Last season ended in disappointment and, although I wasn't here at the time, I know how important it is to bounce back this campaign. As well as on-field matters, we also have a brand new Main Stand here at Tynecastle Park. Our home ground has always been one of the most atmospheric in the country and it will now prove to be even noisier than before. I can't wait to be a part of more memorable matches in front of a packed Tynecastle!

"We have an incredible fan base that backs the club through thick and thin and it is my responsibility to help ensure every Hearts fan has a team they can be proud of."

Within the pages of this annual, you can read all about the history of the Old Main Stand and marvel at some stunning images taken of the Archibald Leitch Stand over the years. There is also a look back at last season, plus player profiles, quizzes, posters, stats and interviews for you to enjoy.

Last, but not least, I want to thank you all for your incredible support!

Christophe Berra

Captain

Main Stand in Numbers

The Archibald Leitch Stand is now consigned to Hearts history, but the memories will live on forever. Below are some key stats relating to the famous Main Stand's 103-year reign in Gorgie.

Top 10 Appearances Competitive Games		P	G
1	**John Robertson** from 1981-82 to 1997-98	323	161
2	**Gary Mackay** from 1980-81 to 1996-97	P319	46
3	**Henry Smith** from 1981-82 to 1995-96	P300	0
4	**Jim Cruickshank** from 1960-61 to 1976-77	P267	0
5	**Alan Anderson** from 1963-64 to 1975-76	P241	19
6	**John Cumming** from 1950-51 to 1966-67	P237	26
7	**Walter Kidd** from 1977-78 to 1990-91	P221	5
8	**Duncan McClure** from 1933-34 to 1947-48	P213	3
9	**Tommy Walker** from 1932-33 to 1948-49	P209	147
	John Colquhoun from 1985-86 to 1996-97	P209	40

Top 10 Goalscorers Competitive Games		P	G
1	**John Robertson** from 1981-82 to 1997-98	323	161
2	**Willie Bauld** from 1948-49 to 1961-62	207	158
3	**Jimmy Wardhaugh** from 1946-47 to 1959-60	205	150
4	**Tommy Walker** from 1932-33 to 1948-49	209	147
5	**Jock White** from 1922-23 to 1933-34	161	132
6	**Alfie Conn Snr** from 1944-45 to 1957-58	168	106
7	**Andy Black** from 1935-36 to 1945-46	96	90
8	**Barney Battles Jnr** from 1928-29 to 1935-36	79	86
9	**Archie Kelly** from 1942-43 to 1947-48	81	66
10	**Willie Wallace** from 1960-61 to 1966-67	117	64
	Donald Ford from 1964-65 to 1975-76	187	64

Top 10 Managers Competitive Games		P	W	D	L	F	A
1	**Tommy Walker** from 1950-51 to 1966-67	342	212	68	62	916	458
2	**William McCartney** from 1919-20 to 1934-35	340	190	82	68	796	388
3	**Alex MacDonald** from 1981-82 to 1990-91	209	115	56	38	370	194
4	**David McLean** from 1940-41 to 1950-51	194	116	32	46	513	285
5	**Jim Jefferies** from 1995-96 to 2011-12	147	74	32	41	246	175
6	**John McCartney** from 1914-15 to 1919-20	97	61	10	26	181	106
7	**Bobby Seith** from 1970-71 to 1974-75	94	40	31	23	129	92
8	**John Harvey** from 1966-67 to 1970-71	92	41	24	27	137	105
9	**Craig Levein** from 2000-01 to 2004-05	84	48	16	20	142	93
	Joe Jordan from 1990-91 to 1992-93	71	44	14	13	107	54

Top 10 Hat Trick Scorers Competitive Games

		HAT TRICKS
1	**Jock White** from 1922-23 to 1933-34	11
	Willie Bauld from 1948-49 to 1959-60	11
3	**Barney Battles Jnr** from 1928-29 to 1933-34	10
	Tommy Walker from 1934-35 to 1943-44	10
	Jimmy Wardhaugh from 1949-50 to 1957-58	10
6	**Andy Black** from 1936-37 to 1944-45	6
	Archie Garrett from 1938-39 to 1943-44	6
	Archie Kelly from 1943-44 to 1945-46	6
	Alfie Conn Snr from 1950-51 to 1955-56	6
10	**Andy Wilson** from 1918-19 to 1918-19	4
	Alex Young from 1955-56 to 1959-60	4
	Willie Wallace from 1962-63 to 1966-67	4

Top 10 Crowds

		CROWD
1	**Sat 13 Feb 1932** Hearts 0 Rangers 1 Scottish Cup R3	53,396
2	**Sat 20 Feb 1926** Hearts 0 Celtic 4 Scottish Cup R3	50,500
3	**Sat 17 Mar 1956** Hearts 1 Rangers 1 Division A 26 of 34	50,000
4	**Sat 03 Sep 1938** Hearts 1 Celtic 5 Division A 05 of 38	49,905
5	**Sat 18 Feb 1939** Hearts 2 Celtic 2 Scottish Cup R3	49,572
6	**Sat 20 Feb 1954** Hearts 3 Rangers 3 Division A 25 of 30	49,000
	Sat 01 Jan 1955 Hearts 5 Hibernian 1 Division A 14 of 30	49,000
	Sat 13 Apr 1957 Hearts 0 Rangers 1 Division 1 32 of 34	49,000
9	**Wed 21 Feb 1934** Hearts 1 Rangers 2 Scottish Cup R3	48,895
10	**Sat 05 Mar 1955** Hearts 1 Aberdeen 1 Scottish Cup QF	48,723

Top 10 Record Scores

			GOALS
1	**Sat 13 Feb 1937**	Hearts 15 Kings Park 0 Scottish Cup R2	15
2	**Sat 04 Feb 1939**	Hearts 14 Elgin City 1 Scottish Cup R2	14
3	**Sat 21 Jan 1939**	Hearts 14 Penicuik Athletic 2 Scottish Cup R1	14
4	**Sat 16 Jan 1932**	Hearts 13 Lochgelly United 3 Scottish Cup R1	13
5	**Sat 28 Feb 2015**	Hearts 10 Cowdenbeath 0 Championship 26 of 36	10
6	**Sat 15 May 1926**	Hearts 9 Leith Athletic 0 Rosebery Charity Cup Final	9
	Sat 28 Feb 1931	Hearts 9 Ayr United 0 Division A 30 of 38	9
	Sat 23 Oct 1943	Hearts 9 Queens Park 0 Wartime S 11 of 30	9
	Sat 12 Nov 1949	Hearts 9 Falkirk 0 Division A 09 of 30	9
	Sat 05 Oct 1957	Hearts 9 East Fife 0 Division 1 04 of 34	9
	Sat 28 Jan 1961	Hearts 9 Tarff Rovers 0 Scottish Cup R1	9

2016/17 Season Review

The Jambos' 2016/17 campaign was very much a tale of two halves. It began with European football in June 2016 as Estonian side FC Infonet were knocked out over two legs before Hearts were themselves eliminated by Birkirkara FC of Malta in the next round.

The Ladbrokes Premiership season began with two defeats and a draw against Celtic, St Johnstone and Aberdeen respectively. Three straight victories followed as Hearts began to pick up where they left off the previous season.

By the time December arrived however, big changes had been made. Hearts defeated Rangers 2-0 at Tynecastle on 30th November, a stunning performance which will also be remembered for being Robbie Neilson's last game in charge of the boys in maroon. The Head Coach and his Assistant Stevie Crawford left to join English League One side MK Dons shortly after, with Ian Cathro and Austin MacPhee coming in to replace them.

The start of 2017 saw no less than nine new players arrive, with the likes of Igor Rossi, Robbie Muirhead and Alim Öztürk departing. Such a large changeover in personnel inevitably had an effect on performances and the latter half of the season didn't quite live up to expectations, although there were some impressive performances to be had.

The team ended the season in fifth place and over the next few pages we look back at five of the games of the Jambos' 2016/17 season. During the summer of 2017, Ian Cathro left Hearts and Craig Levein was appointed Manager in August.

Fixtures / Results / Goals

League / Cup	Day	Date	Opponent	H/A	Score	Crowd	Goal scorers
Europa Q	Thu	Jun 30	**Fc Infonet**	H	2-1	14419	Buaben (pen) / Kalimullin (og)
Europa Q	Wed	Jun 6	**Fc Infonet**	A	4-2	1354	Paterson / Rossi 2 / Ozturk
Europa Q	Thu	Jun 14	**Birkirkara**	A	0-0	1868	
Europa Q	Thu	Jun 21	**Birkirkara**	H	1-2	14301	Sammon
Premiership	Sun	Aug 7	**Celtic**	H	1-2	16777	Walker (pen)
L Cup 2	Wed	Aug 10	**St Johnstone**	A	2-3	4214	Paterson / Walker (pen)
Premiership	Sat	Aug 13	**Aberdeen**	A	0-0	13559	
Premiership	Sat	Aug 20	**Inverness Ct**	H	5-1	15880	Cowie 2 / Sammon / Nicholson 2
Premiership	Sat	Aug 27	**Partick Thistle**	A	2-1	4919	Paterson / Watt
Premiership	Sat	Sep 10	**Hamilton**	H	3-1	15947	Walker 2 (1 pen) / Nicholson
Premiership	Sat	Sep 17	**St Johnstone**	A	0-1	5465	
Premiership	Sat	Sep 24	**Ross County**	H	0-0	16321	
Premiership	Fri	Sep 30	**Motherwell**	A	3-1	4666	Mcmanus (og) / Paterson / Djoum
Premiership	Sat	Oct 15	**Dundee**	H	2-0	16512	Paterson / Johnsen
Premiership	Wed	Oct 26	**Kilmarnock**	A	0-2	3917	
Premiership	Sat	Oct 29	**Inverness Ct**	A	3-3	3565	Johnsen / Rherras / Djoum
Premiership	Sat	Nov 5	**St Johnstone**	H	2-2	16421	Buaben / Paterson
Premiership	Mon	Nov 21	**Hamilton**	A	3-3	2339	Walker 2 (1 pen) / Paterson
Premiership	Sat	Nov 26	**Motherwell**	H	3-0	16199	Johnsen 2 / Walker
Premiership	Wed	Nov 30	**Rangers**	H	2-0	16803	Muirhead 2
Premiership	Sat	Dec 3	**Ross County**	A	2-2	4042	Djoum / Paterson
Premiership	Sat	Dec 10	**Rangers**	A	0-2	50039	
Premiership	Sat	Dec 17	**Partick Thistle**	H	1-1	16418	Johnsen
Premiership	Fri	Dec 23	**Dundee**	A	2-3	6160	Walker (pen) / Paterson
Premiership	Tue	Dec 27	**Kilmarnock**	H	4-0	16696	Paterson / Djoum / Walker 2
Premiership	Frid	Dec 30	**Aberdeen**	H	0-1	16630	
SFA Cup 4	Sun	Jan 22	**Raith Rovers**	A	1-1	5036	Walker
Replay	Wed	Jan 25	**Raith Rovers**	H	4-2	10740	Currie / Martin (pen) / Walker (pen) / Johnsen
Premiership	Sun	Jan 29	**Celtic**	A	0-4	58247	
Premiership	Wed	Feb 1	**Rangers**	H	4-1	16570	Nowak / Walker 2 / Cowie
Premiership	Sat	Feb 4	**Motherwell**	A	3-0	4651	Tziolis / Goncalves 2
SFA Cup 5	Sun	Feb 12	**Hibernian**	H	0-0	16971	
Premiership	Sat	Feb 18	**Inverness Ct**	H	1-1	16372	Djoum
SFA Cup Replay	Wed	Feb 22	**Hibernian**	A	1-3	20205	Goncalves
Premiership	Sat	Feb 25	**Partick Thistle**	A	0-2	4143	
Premiership	Wed	Mar 1	**Ross County**	H	0-1	15470	
Premiership	Sat	Feb 11	**Hamilton**	H	4-0	15881	Djoum / Goncalves / Walker / Martin
Premiership	Sat	Feb 18	**Aberdeen**	A	0-2	12178	
Premiership	Sun	Apr 2	**Celtic**	H	0-5	16539	
Premiership	Wed	Apr 5	**St Johnstone**	A	0-1	4197	
Premiership	Sat	Apr 8	**Dundee**	H	1-0	16304	Goncalves
Premiership	Frid	Apr 14	**Kilmarnock**	A	0-0	4110	
Premiership	Sat	Apr 29	**Partick Thistle**	H	2-2	15930	Goncalves / Struna
Premiership	Sun	May 7	**Aberdeen**	H	1-2	16522	Goncalves
Premiership	Sat	May 13	**Rangers**	A	1-2	47809	Goncalves
Premiership	Wed	May 17	**St Johnstone**	A	0-1	3141	
Premiership	Sun	May 21	**Celtic**	A	0-2	58967	

5 OF THE BEST!

Hearts 5-1 Inverness Caledonian Thistle

Hearts were still searching for their first domestic win of the season when they welcomed Inverness CT to Tynecastle on August 20th.

This proved to be the day they kick-started their campaign as they put five goals past the Highlanders at a rain soaked Tynecastle.

The three preceding games had seen Hearts lose to Celtic at Tynecastle on the opening day before going down 3-2 at McDiarmid Park in the League Cup. That was followed up by a 0-0 draw away to Aberdeen and the boys in maroon were determined to return to winning ways at the fourth time of asking.

Robbie Neilson received a pre-match boost with the news that summer signing Bjørn Johnsen's transfer had finally gone through, meaning the towering striker could take his place among the substitutes and potentially make his Hearts debut in front of the Tynecastle faithful.

The Jambos made one change from the side that drew at Pittodrie, with Perry Kitchen slotting in for Prince Buaben.

It took Hearts only seven minutes to get their noses in front and it came courtesy of the skipper. Cowie dummied a John Souttar pass and spun away to get on the receiving end of Conor Sammon's lay off, and the midfield maestro beautifully curled an effort beyond Owain Fôn Williams from the edge of the box.

It was then nearly 2-0 on 12 minutes. Sammon's flick-on saw Tony Watt bully his way through the Caley defence and drill a low shot on target but it was straight at Fôn Williams, who made a smart block with his legs and clawed the ball behind at the second attempt.

The second goal did eventually arrive after 17 minutes and it was for the men in maroon. Watt showed great skill to retain possession inside the Caley Thistle box and knocked it sideways for Cowie to loop a cross to the back door where Sammon rose highest to head back across goals and into an empty net.

Hearts continued to boss the play, impressing on the attack and looking solid in defence. Cowie's 35th minute free-kick found Paterson in the box but his glancing header was straight at Fôn Williams.

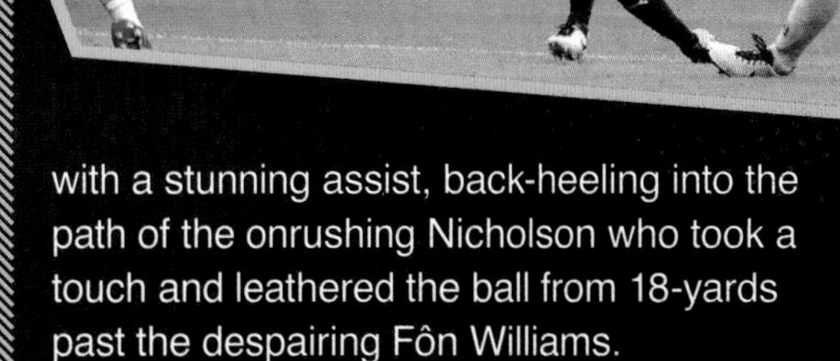

The visitors fluffed a great chance to pull one back three minutes later when Liam Polworth weaved his way through the Hearts defence to find Scott Boden unmarked in the box, however the striker snatched at it and ballooned his effort well wide of the target.

The Jambos started the second half with a bang, making it 3-0 two minutes in with a near carbon copy of the game's first goal. This time Watt drove forward before playing a pass into the box for Sammon to tee up Cowie to curl in his second, and Hearts' third, of the game.

The Gorgie boys were then denied what looked like a stonewall penalty when Sam Nicholson was tripped inside the box by Gary Warren as he shaped up to shoot, but referee Steven MacLean waved play on.

Substitute Alex Fisher made an instant impact with a spectacular overhead kick inside the Hearts box but Jack Hamilton pounced to his right to push the ball around the post.

Cowie was a man on a mission, looking to grab his hat-trick. Watt again showed great build up play and Cowie managed to create space for himself inside the box to pull off a shot but a deflection from a Caley Thistle defender carried the ball over the bar.

Johnsen was then introduced late in the second half and set up Hearts' fourth goal with a stunning assist, back-heeling into the path of the onrushing Nicholson who took a touch and leathered the ball from 18-yards past the despairing Fôn Williams.

A minute later it was 5-0. Cowie's defence-splitting pass found Nicholson and the winger coolly ran through on goal and knocked it past the Caley 'keeper, despite Fôn Williams getting a hand to it, and into the back of the net.

The visitors stole a consolation goal with three minutes remaining when a loose ball was poked home by Draper, despite Paterson's best attempts on the line, but it gave the Jambos a familiar 5-1 winning scoreline after what was a commanding performance in Gorgie.

5 OF THE BEST!

30/11/16

Hearts 2-0 Rangers

Hearts ran out comfortable 2-0 winners over Rangers on a magical night at Tynecastle.

A brace from Robbie Muirhead was enough to give the Jambos all three points in front of a sell-out crowd in Gorgie, in a match where Hearts were magnificent from start to finish.

Robbie Neilson named an unchanged team after the previous Saturday's thumping 3-0 win over Motherwell.

The game started at breakneck speed with an electric atmosphere swaying around the ground. The Jambos had the upper hand in the early possession stakes and in the 9th minute Bjørn Johnsen rose magnificently to flick on Callum Paterson's throw in, but Muirhead couldn't connect quick enough at the back post.

Rangers threatened in the 14th minute when Jason Holt carried the ball forward before squaring to James Tavernier, who struck a sweet shot over the bar from 25-yards out.

The game then got slightly scrappy but still the men in maroon enjoyed the lion's share of possession. Jamie Walker twisted and turned deep inside the Rangers box in the 32nd minute and pulled off a shot at goal but it was straight into the arms of Wes Foderingham.

Paterson was next to try his luck, brilliantly spinning away from his man to advance to the edge of the box and rifle a shot on target, only to see Foderingham block the ball away.

Moments later Hearts threatened again. Paterson was fouled by Kenny Miller, and Muirhead's free-kick was nodded goalwards by Johnsen, but straight at Foderingham.

With five minutes to go until half-time, the Jambos had the best chance of the match. Paterson's long throw into the box was met by Johnsen, whose bullet header looked to be creeping in under the bar, but Foderingham managed to expertly tip it over the bar.

Johnsen was in the thick of it and nearly created a chance for himself out of nothing. Faycal Rherras' cross into the box looked to be bread and butter for the Rangers defence but Johnsen somehow managed to pluck the ball out of the air, only to see Foderingham rush off his line to smother the ball.

The deadlock was broken in the 44th minute deservedly by Hearts. Johnsen's brilliant flick saw Djoum run in on goal but was forced to knock back to the American, whose teasing ball across the face of goal was met by Muirhead who slid to slam beyond Foderingham and into the back of the net.

There was still time before the half was out for Jack Hamilton to be called into action, diving to his left to keep out a deflected Andy Halliday effort.

Hearts started the second-half on the front foot, with Walker holding off his man at the edge of the box to shoot, but he scuffed his effort and Fotheringham gathered with ease.

Rangers thought they had equalised in the 51st minute. Miller's long-range shot was palmed out by Hamilton but Dodoo took a touch inside the box and slammed into the net, however Harry Forrester was standing in front of the Hearts 'keeper, blocking his view, and the linesman flagged for offside.

The Jambos went straight up the park and nearly doubled their lead. Johnsen carried the ball into the box and drilled a shot on goal from an acute angle but Foderingham did well to turn it around the post.

Tyencastle erupted once again just before the hour mark when Hearts doubled their lead. Arnaud Djoum sent Walker down the right and his ball to the back post was met by Muirhead, who once again slammed into the net for his and Hearts' second of the game.

Foderingham was at his best three minutes later to deny Hearts a third. John Souttar went on a mazy run that took to the edge of the box and his deft pass found Johnsen, whose low effort was palmed away by the Rangers 'keeper.

Hearts really should've had the chance to make it three from the spot when substitute Michael O'Halloran stamped on Rherras' heels when clean through on goal, but referee Craig Thomson said no.

It didn't matter in the end, as Rangers couldn't get near the Gorgie Boys and three points took them up into second place in the Ladbrokes Premiership table.

5 OF THE BEST!

27/12/16

Hearts 4-0 Kilmarnock

Hearts ran riot against Kilmarnock at Tynecastle, putting 4-0 past the Ayshire side without reply.

The Jambos bulldozed their opponents from first whistle 'til last, with the three points coming from Callum Paterson and Arnaud Djoum strikes, plus a brace from Jamie Walker.

Ian Cathro made two changes to the side that narrowly lost at Dens Park four days prior. Faycal Rherras replaced Liam Smith while Prince Buaben came in for the injured Don Cowie.

Despite Hearts seeing most of the ball in the opening stages it was Kilmarnock who nearly took the lead inside five minutes. Kris Boyd latched onto a long ball but Jack Hamilton was quick enough off his line to get a touch on it and the ball ricocheted off the striker's hand and onto the goalline for Igor Rossi to clear.

Three minutes later Hearts took the lead. Jamie Walker's corner was only cleared to the edge of the box and Paterson hit a stunning volley on the turn that flew past Jamie MacDonald and into the bottom corner of the net.

Hearts were dealt a massive blow on 15 minutes when goalscorer Paterson was stretchered off with a leg injury; he was replaced by Liam Smith. Moments before, Souleymane Coulibaly glanced a free header wide of the target.

It was nearly 2-0 after 19 minutes. Walker's low corner was flicked goalwards by Bjørn Johnsen but, while the American's header beat Macdonald, Martin Smith popped up on the line to clear the danger.

The second goal did come for Hearts, perhaps somewhat fortuitously, after 42 minutes. Liam Smith's looping cross into the Killie box found Djoum, who had beaten the offside trap, and the ball hit off the Cameroon international as he lunged for it and spun into the back of the net.

Hearts started the second-half brightly when Walker let the ball run across him at the edge of the box before turning to shoot, but couldn't find the target.

Walker made no mistake in the 48th minute. A shanked clearance from Walker's corner found Buaben 20-yards out and his low drive was palmed back into the six-yard box by MacDonald, and Hearts no.7 was quickest with the follow up to slam home from close range to give the Jambos a commanding 3-0 lead.

Djoum tested MacDonald with a diving header from Walker's free-kick on the hour mark, but the Killie 'keeper produced a good diving save to beat the ball away.

It should've been 4-0 three minutes later. Johnsen's flick on saw Walker run onto the ball and take it around MacDonald but Iain Wilson made a superb last-ditch tackle when the winger looked odds-on to score.

From the resultant corner Johnsen connected with his head but could only flash the ball wide of the target.

Hearts put the game completely to bed in the 70th minute. Boyle's poor backpass was latched onto by Walker who had all the time in the world to run it into the box and drill low past MacDonald to make it 4-0.

The men in maroon were rampant by this point, with skipper Perry Kitchen getting in on the action. He picked up a loose ball in the 76th minute and drove forward, playing a neat one-two with Djoum before shooting low, but MacDonald got down to make the save.

Cathro's side weren't finished there and were only denied a fifth by the woodwork. Krystian Nowak curled a beautiful effort from 25-yards that beat MacDonald but crashed off his left-hand post.

Moments later the Pole's header from substitute Robbie Muirhead's corner was cleared off the line by Coulibaly.

The onslaught kept on coming, with Muirhead jinking forward and trying his luck from outside the box, but he could only drag his effort wide.

Deep into stoppage time Hearts were awarded a penalty after substitute Dario Zanatta was barged over inside the box, but the young Canadian saw his spot kick stopped by MacDonald.

A thoroughly deserved win for Hearts.

01/02/17

Hearts 4-1 Rangers

Hearts cruised to a 4-1 victory against Rangers under the Tynecastle floodlights.

Krystian Nowak gave the Jambos an early lead but the visitors struck back through Emerson Hyndman. A second-half blitz saw Don Cowie and a Jamie Walker double seal the win in style.

Ian Cathro made three changes to the side that lost out at Celtic Park four days previously. Struna returned from injury to replace Liam Smith, long-term absentee John Souttar missed out and Nowak came in, while Isma Gonçalves was handed his debut for Sam Nicholson.

The Jambos got off to a flying start, opening the scoring in three minutes. Perry Kitchen's quick free-kick down the line allowed Struna to float a ball into the box for Nowak to leap highest and power a header into the opposite corner of the net.

Three minutes later it was nearly 2-0. Malaury Martin drilled a free-kick low from 20-yards that flew past everyone inside the box and narrowly beyond Wes Foderingham's left-hand post.

Martin went close again in the 9th minute, after Isma was bundled to the ground by Clint Hill on the edge of the box. The Frenchman stepped up and curled an effort inches wide of the target.

Jack Hamilton had to be alert in the 15th minute when Martyn Waghorn cut inside from the left to fire a low shot on target, but the Hearts No.1 did well to beat the ball away.

A brace of long-range Kitchen efforts saw the skipper fire wide and over respectively, as Hearts were dominating proceedings by the 23rd minute.

There was a real heart-in-mouth moment when Nowak erroneously passed back to Waghorn inside the box, but Hamilton did well to close the angle and make a block on the byline.

Rangers were starting to come back into the game by the half-hour mark, with Barrie McKay's swerving shot from the edge of the box dipping past Hamilton's left-hand post.

Disaster struck in the 35th minute when Rangers equalised. James Tavernier's corner was punched to the middle of the box but Hyndman was on hand to lash home high into the roof of the net.

The visitors went close again before the half was out when Hyndman managed to hold off Aaron Hughes inside the box to pull off a shot, but Hamilton tipped the ball over the bar.

Just like the beginning of the game, Hearts started the second-half with a bang. Walker robbed Halliday of possession 25-yards out and carried it forward a few yards before blasting low beyond Hamilton to give the men in maroon the lead.

It was 3-1 after 54 minutes. A quick free-kick sent Bjørn Johnsen free down the left, he cut inside and drilled across the six-yard box for Cowie to tap into an empty net.

Hearts were playing with their tails up again, with substitute Alex Tziolis looping a cross into the box for Walker to hit a spectacular volley, only to see the ball spin wide.

By the 63rd minute Hearts had scored their fourth. Cowie's high cross into the box was misjudged by Foderingham – under pressure from Johnsen – and the ball fell perfectly for Walker to knock home for his brace.

Incredibly, it could've been 5-1 four minutes later. Walker bore down on goal and looked set to pull the trigger but Tavernier pulled off a great last-ditch tackle to send the ball behind.

Rangers had the ball in the back of the net when substitute Harry Forrester bundled over the line after Hamilton had saved from Jason Holt, but the Rangers man was flagged offside.

Walker was close to grabbing a hat-trick in the 78th minute with a stunning free-kick, but Foderingham flung himself across his goals to stop the winger's curling effort.

From the resultant corner the ball broke to Lennard Sowah 30-yards out and the left-back's thunderbolt was superbly tipped over the bar by Foderingham.

5 OF THE BEST!

Motherwell 0-3 Hearts

Hearts were comfortable 3-0 winners against Motherwell at Fir Park.

The Jambos won it thanks to an Isma Gonçalves brace, after Alex Tziolis had put the Gorgie boys in front.

Ian Cathro made two changes from the side that defeated Rangers in midweek. The Greek duo of Tasos Avlonitis and Tziolis were handed their first starts for the club, with Krystian Nowak and Perry Kitchen moving to the bench.

Hearts had their first chance after only four minutes. Isma picked up possession and carried it forward before drilling low from 20-yards out, narrowly missing the target.

There was a scare three minutes later when Louis Moult headed Chris Cadden's cross off the bar and down onto the line, but the linesman flagged for offside.

Jamie Walker showed great tenacity to rob Zak Jules of possession then stay on his feet as the defender brought him down; he then blasted inches over from 25-yards out.

Walker was in the mix again on 21 minutes, driving into the Motherwell box before sending Lennard Sowah clear down the left, he cut back for the winger who hit the side netting from 15-yards.

Malaury Martin forced Craig Samson into a good save in the 29th minute, curling a set piece from 25-yards on target, but the Well 'keeper got down to turn the ball around his left-hand post.

Despite Hearts dominating the game it was the hosts who nearly took the lead five minutes before half time. A corner in was only cleared to the edge of the box and Lionel Ainsworth shot low, only for Avlonitis to clear off the line.

Moult then followed that up with a superb curling free-kick from the edge of the box that flew just wide of Jack Hamilton's left-hand post.

Bjørn Johnsen stayed indoors at the start of the second-half, replaced by Choulay as

Hearts went in search of the goal that their play richly deserved.

Seven minutes into the restart Motherwell were reduced to ten men. Carl McHugh went over the ball when challenging Don Cowie, and referee Andrew Dallas showed no hesitation in flashing the red.

Hearts made the breakthrough on 59 minutes and it was courtesy of Tziolis. The Greek midfielder picked up possession 25-yards out and lashed an effort that looped over Samson and into the net, via a deflection off a home shirt.

Motherwell kept battling and nearly got an equaliser in the 66th minute. A free-kick was cleared only as far as the edge of the box and Keith Lasley 's first-time shot dropped inches wide of the post.

It was so nearly 2-0 three minutes later. A series of quick passes deep inside the Motherwell half saw Sowah break free down the left to cut back for Gonçalves, but his turn and shot landed the wrong side of the post.

Gonçalves had another effort on goal, brushing past two Motherwell players and into the box but fired straight at Samson.

With five minutes remaining Hearts put the game to bed. A quick breakaway saw Choulay slip through Isma, and the hitman slotted low beyond Samson to make it 2-0.

Not content with two, the Jambos bagged a third with two minutes to go. Choulay won possession on the right to square it to Isma, and Portuguese striker slammed home his second of the game to give Hearts a comfortable victory.

Pre-Season

Fighting Fit

In preparation for the 2017/18 season, the Hearts first team squad travelled to Ireland for a week long training camp.

The team jetted out to Dublin from Edinburgh on July 3rd and set up base at a hotel resort within a 40 minute drive of the Irish capital. Top notch training facilities were located within the grounds of the hotel, enabling the team to undertake double training sessions as they worked on their fitness and shape ahead of the new season.

On Wednesday July 5th they faced St Patrick's Athletic in Dublin for a friendly match that ended in a 1-0 defeat.

The Jambos took the opportunity to give just about every player game time and it was deemed a worthwhile workout despite the one goal loss.

The team spent the next day training back at their hotel base before journeying north to Belfast on the Friday ahead of a friendly against Linfield on Saturday afternoon.

The match was played at Windsor Park, the home of Northern Ireland's national team, and attracted several hundred Hearts fans who witnessed their side run out convincing 4-1 winners. 16-year-old Harry Cochrane opened the scoring for Hearts before Jamie Walker, Isma and Cole Stockton completed the rout.

Player Profiles

JACK HAMILTON
GOALKEEPER

DOB: 22.03.94

Previous Club(s):
Stenhousemuir

VIKTOR NORING
GOALKEEPER

DOB: 03.02.91

Previous Club(s):
Trelleborgs, Malmö, Celtic, Bodø/Glimt, Heerenveen, Lyngby BK

JON MCLAUGHLIN
GOALKEEPER

DOB: 09.09.87

Previous Club(s):
Harrogate Town, Bradford City, Burton Albion

MICHAEL SMITH
DEFENDER

DOB: 04.09.88

Previous Club(s):
Ballyclare Comrades, Ballymena Utd, Bristol Rovers, Peterborough

LIAM SMITH
DEFENDER

DOB: 10.04.96

Previous Club(s):
East Fife (loan), Raith Rovers (loan)

JAMIE BRANDON
DEFENDER

DOB: 05.02.98

Previous Club(s):
Rangers

KRYSTIAN NOWAK

DEFENDER

DOB: 01.04.94

Previous Club(s):
UKS SMS Łódź, Tur Turek, Widzew Łódź, Podbeskidzie Bielsko-Biała

AARON HUGHES

DEFENDER

DOB: **08.11.79**

Previous Club(s):
Newcastle Utd, Aston Villa, Fulham, QPR, Brighton, Melbourne City, Kerala Blasters

JOHN SOUTTAR

DEFENDER

DOB: **25.09.96**

Previous Club(s):
Dundee Utd

CHRISTOPHE BERRA

DEFENDER

DOB: **31.01.85**

Previous Club(s):
Wolverhampton Wanderers, Ipswich Town

ASHLEY SMITH-BROWN

DEFENDER

DOB: **31.03.96**

Previous Club(s):
Manchester City, NAC Breda

RAFAL GRZELĄK

DEFENDER

DOB: **07.08.88**

Previous Club(s): **Wisła Płock, Dolcan Ząbki, Podbeskidzie Bielsko-Biała, Korona Kielce**

MALAURY MARTIN

MIDFIELDER

DOB: 25.08.88

Previous Club(s):
Monaco, Blackpool, Middlesbrough, Lausanne-Sport, Sandnes Ulf, Lillestrøm

DON COWIE

MIDFIELDER

DOB: 15.02.83

Previous Club(s):
Ross County, Inverness CT, Watford, Cardiff City, Wigan Athletic

ARNAUD DJOUM

MIDFIELDER

DOB: 02.05.89

Previous Club(s):
Brussels, Anderlecht, Roda JC, Akhisar Belediyespor, Lech Poznań

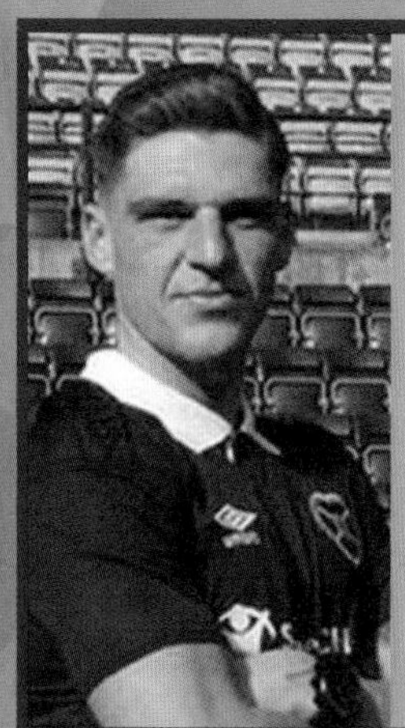

ROSS CALLACHAN

MIDFIELDER

DOB: 04.09.93

Previous clubs:
Raith Rovers

JAMIE WALKER

MIDFIELDER

DOB: 25.06.93

Previous Club(s): **N/A**

CONNOR RANDALL

MIDFIELDER

DOB: 21.10.96

Previous Club(s):
Liverpool

ANGUS BEITH

MIDFIELDER

DOB: 22.02.96

Previous Club(s): **N/A**

PRINCE BUABEN

MIDFIELDER

DOB: 23.04.88

Previous Club(s):
Dundee Utd, Watford, Carlisle Utd, Partick Thistle

MARCUS GODINHO

MIDFIELDER

DOB: 28.06.97

Previous Club(s):
Toronto FC,
Vaughan Azzurri

MANUEL MILINKOVIC

MIDFIELDER

DOB: 20.05.94

Previous clubs:
Salernitana, Ternana,
Genoa, Foggia

DARIO ZANATTA

MIDFIELDER

DOB: 24.05.97

Previous Club(s):
Vancouver Whitecaps

RORY CURRIE

STRIKER

DOB: 20.02.98

Previous Club(s): Rangers

ESMAEL GONCALVES

STRIKER

DOB: 25.06.91

Previous Club(s):
Nice, Rio Ave, St Mirren,
APOEL, Veria, Anorthosis
Famagusta, Ettifaq FC

COLE STOCKTON

STRIKER

DOB: 13.03.94

Previous Club(s):
Tranmere Rovers,
Vauxhall Motors,
Southport, Morecambe

KYLE LAFFERTY

STRIKER

DOB: 16.09.87

Previous Club(s): Burnley,
Darlington, Rangers,
Sion, Palermo, Norwich
City, Çaykur Rizespor,
Birmingham City

Back in Maroon

Hearts' first move ahead of the 2017/18 season was to bring **Christophe Berra** home to Tynecastle.

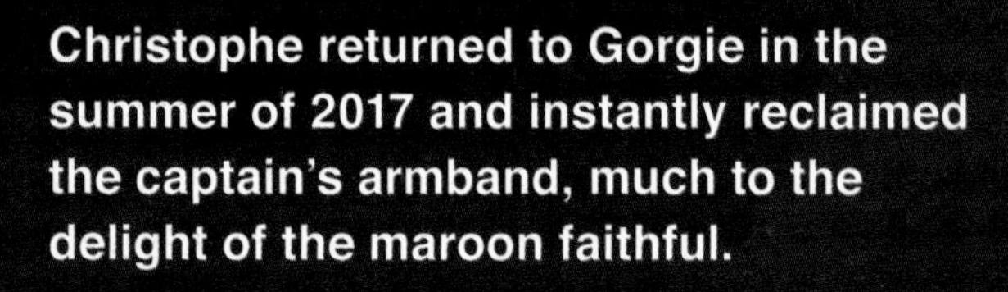

Christophe returned to Gorgie in the summer of 2017 and instantly reclaimed the captain's armband, much to the delight of the maroon faithful.

The Edinburgh-born defender began his career at Hearts, emerging from the club's youth system before making his breakthrough into the first team in 2003 at the age of 18. He made his debut as a substitute in a 2-1 defeat to Dundee United in November 2003 before truly establishing himself as a first team regular during the 2005/06 campaign.

It proved to be a memorable season in Gorgie as Hearts went on to lift the Scottish Cup after defeating Gretna on penalties. Christophe was an unused substitute that day but he was already making his mark and duly signed a five year deal with the club that summer. In 2007 he was appointed club captain before going on to win his first Scotland cap in a 3-1 friendly defeat to Czech Republic in 2008.

By that point, Christophe's consistent performances were attracting plenty of potential suitors and Hearts eventually agreed to let him go in January 2009. English Championship Wolverhampton Wanderers side paid an undisclosed fee to bring the towering defender, who had made 146 competitive appearances for Hearts, to the Molineux stadium.

Christophe's influence helped his new club seal promotion to the English Premiership and he established himself as a mainstay in the side that spent three seasons in England's top-flight. He made no less

"I've been away for a long time now and I always had it in the back of my mind that I wanted to come back here. I missed playing at Tynecastle."

than 154 appearances for Wolves before leaving to join Ipswich Town in July 2013.

His skill, work ethic and passion ensured he quickly adhered himself to the Trotters' support, resulting in him being named the club's Player of the Year in 2013/14. He continued to be a key player for the Portman Road side right up to the end of the 2016/17 season, when he made it clear that he wished to return to Scotland.

Christophe's desire to return north alerted his boyhood club and on May 23rd it was announced he had sealed his return to Tynecastle on a three year deal at the age of 32. Needless to say, he was welcomed back with open arms by Hearts supporters and making him captain was a no-brainer in the eyes of many.

Upon arriving back in his home city, Christophe was keen to explain how much it means to him to be back in maroon:

"People say that you should never go back a second time. I've been away for a long time now and I always had it in the back of my mind that I wanted to come back here. I missed playing at Tynecastle. I'm a local lad, I grew up here, I know the city, all my friends are here and I know what it means to play for this club. There's no place like home."

Christophe returned to Hearts as a seasoned international footballer and, within weeks of signing, he went on to win his 36th cap for Scotland in the thrilling 2-2 draw with England at Hampden Park.

"I'm a local lad, I grew up here, I know the city, all my friends are here and I know what it means to play for this club. There's no place like home."

Jock's Quiz

Fancy yourself as a bit of a know-it-all when it comes to the boys in maroon? Jock the Jambo's got a few testing questions lined up for you...

1. Who was named Hearts captain ahead of the 2017/18 season?
2. Which Hearts player won the Africa Cup of Nations with Cameroon earlier this year?
3. Aaron Hughes made his professional debut at which famous stadium; San Siro or Nou Camp?
4. The Archibald Leitch Stand was demolished this summer. How old was it?
5. Which former Hearts player scored the most competitive goals in front of the Main Stand?
6. This season sees Hearts' beloved stadium revert to its old name. What is it?
7. Which team did Kyle Lafferty score his first competitive Hearts goal against; Elgin City or East Fife?
8. Hearts' Assistant Coach Austin MacPhee is also part of the coaching setup for which national team?
9. Isma Goncalves previously played for which Scottish club?

10. 2018 will mark the 20 year anniversary of Hearts' 1998 Scottish Cup win. Who did they beat in the final?

Answers on **Page 60**

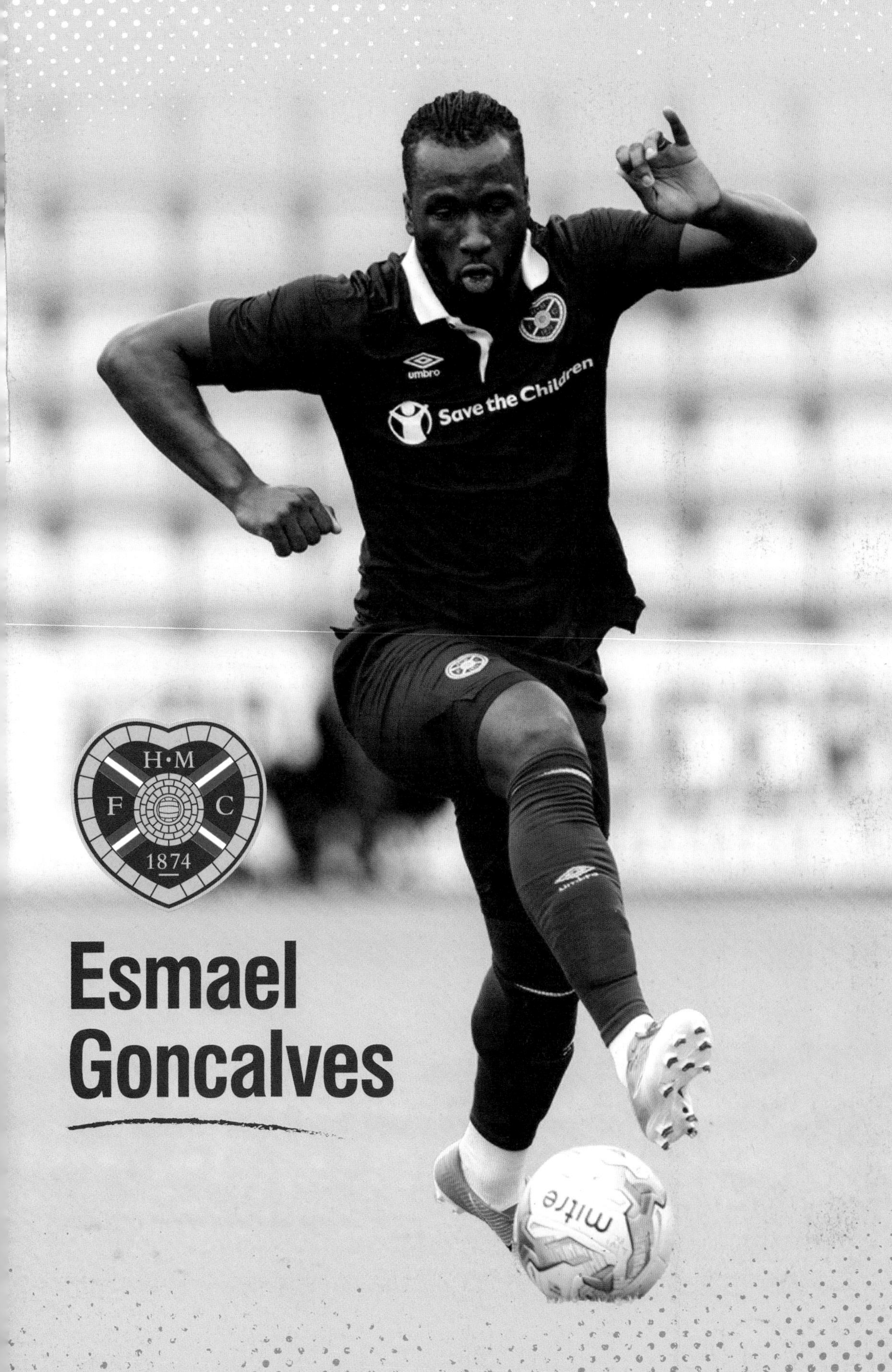

Esmael Goncalves

Hearts Puzzles

Find the words in the grid. Words can go horizontally, vertically and diagonally in all eight directions.

- BERRA
- COWIE
- EDINBURGH
- GONCALVES
- GORGIE
- HUGHES
- LAFFERTY
- MAROON
- STOCKTON
- TYNECASTLE

Hearts Crossword

ACROSS

3 Midfielder from Cameroon (6,5)

5 Wears the number 9 jersey (4,8)

6 Hearts' all-time leading goalscorer (4,9)

DOWN

1 Hearts' owner (3,5)

2 Hearts' mascot (4,3,5)

3 Ex-Newcastle United defender (5,6)

4 Hearts' Manager (5,6)

Answers on **Page 61**

Spot the difference

The photo shows Hearts playing Linfield in July 2017, but can you spot the 10 differences between the two images?

Answers on **Page 61**

Challenge the Goalie

1. Who is Hearts' all-time leading goalscorer?

Robbo

2. What year was the club founded?

1874

3. Name the manager who won the 2012 Scottish Cup with Hearts?

Paulo Sergio

4. Austin MacPhee was previously Assistant Manager at which Championship club?

St Mirren

5. Who is the all-time English Premier League topscorer?

Wayne Rooney

6. Which club plays its home games at Fratton Park?

Portsmouth

7. What Spanish city does Rayo Vallecano come from?

Vallecano?

8. Who won last season's Europa League?

Man Utd

9. Who played in the Scottish Cup final last season?

Celtic and Aberdeen

Can you beat Jack?

Write in your answers to the questions below and find out if you know more than Jack!

10. How many Scotland caps does Don Cowie have: 9, 10 or 11?

10

11. Which Dutch club did Prince Buaben play for before joining Dundee United?

Ajax

12. True or False: Christophe Berra has never scored for Scotland?

False

13. What club does John Souttar's brother play for?

Stoke City

14. What is the capital of Spain?

Pass!

15. What colour of jersey is worn by the leader of the Tour de France?

Yellow and Red

16. What is sushi traditionally wrapped in?

Seaweed

17. What nationality is Justin Bieber?

Canadian

Bonus Question

(1 point per correct answer)

18. Name the three former England managers that Aaron Hughes has played for during his career

Bobby Robson. Steve McClaren maybe? That's all I've got.

Total Scores

Jack	
Your name	

Answers on **Page 60**

Player of the Year Awards

Main Stand Memory
John Robertson

Young Player of the Year and Goal of season
Calum Paterson

The host for the evening, "the voice of Hearts" Scott Wilson, took to the stage to kick off proceedings and the first award of the night, the Doc Melvin Memorial Award, went to the dynamic duo of Jim and Alison Ross.

The Celebration of Youth Awards saw Euan Henderson crowned U17s Player of the Year, with Rory Currie named U20s Player of the Year. The Overall Young Player of the Year Award, as voted for by the first team and U20 squad, went to Callum Paterson.

Club stalwart and current Head of Pro Recruitment, John Murray, picked up the George Nicolson Award.

Elsewhere, Arnaud Djoum received the Special Recognition Award for his outstanding Africa Cup of Nations success with Cameroon earlier this year.

The Main Stand Memory Award went to club legend John Robertson who has made the most competitive appearances (323) in front of the Archibald Leitch Stand. In his acceptance speech Robbo expressed his honour at picking up the award and admitted that, although he would miss the old stand at Tynecastle, he was incredibly excited about the opening of the new Main Stand and all the positives that come with it.

Players, staff and supporters of Heart of Midlothian once again gathered at the EICC on Sunday 23rd April for the club's Player of the Year Awards ceremony

U20 Player of the Year
Rory Currie

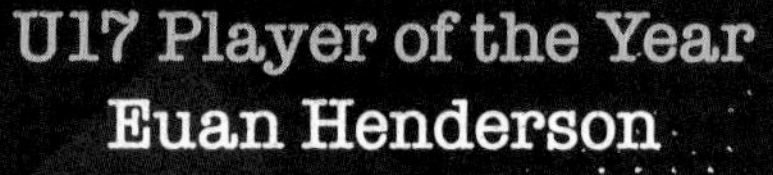

U17 Player of the Year
Euan Henderson

Special Recognition
Arnaud Djoum

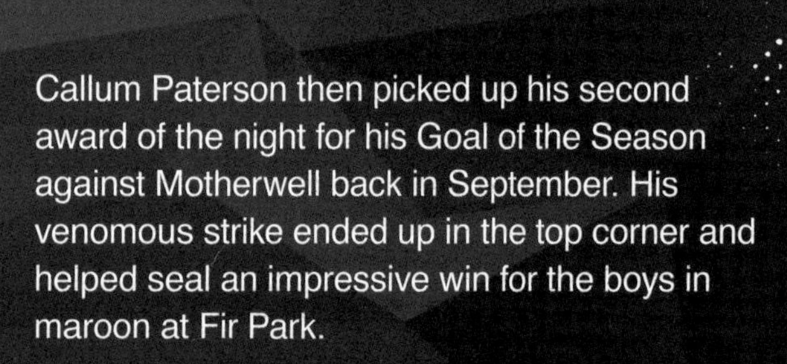

Callum Paterson then picked up his second award of the night for his Goal of the Season against Motherwell back in September. His venomous strike ended up in the top corner and helped seal an impressive win for the boys in maroon at Fir Park.

The second double winner was Jamie Walker who was voted both Fans' Player of the Year and Players' Player of the Year. The fans' favourite finished the season with 15 goals to his name and once again proved hugely influential from his attacking midfield position.

Players' Player of the Year
and Fans' Player of the Year
Jamie Walker

Ones to Watch

Jamie Brandon

Jamie joined the Jambos from Rangers in the summer of 2016 and quickly established himself as a key member of Jon Daly's U20 squad.

The energetic midfielder can also be deployed at right back and that is exactly how he was utilised when Ian Cathro handed him his senior debut on the final day of the 2016/17 league campaign. The venue was Celtic Park but the youngster handled the occasion with great maturity. He also formed part of the first team's 2017/18 pre-season preparations where he continued to play as a right wing back.

Hard-working and assured in possession, Jamie possesses great technical ability and will fancy his chances of breaking into the first team squad on a permanent basis.

Euan Henderson

Having been a stand-out player in the Hearts U17 set-up for a number of seasons, Euan was one of eight youngsters who found themselves rewarded with a full time contract ahead of the 2017/18 season.

The attacking midfielder cuts a powerful shape on the pitch, with blistering pace to match. He is particularly effective in wide areas but his ability to cut inside means he is a constant menace to opposition defences. Like Jamie Brandon, he too made his senior Hearts debut at Celtic Park on the final day of the 2016/17 season and one gets the feeling there will be many more appearances to follow.

The Hearts Academy at Riccarton is home to many a talented young player across various age levels. **Regardless of their age or stage of development, they all share the dream of breaking into the Hearts first team. Here are four players fans can expect to see more of in the coming years...**

Harry Cochrane

Harry is also one of the eight youth players who made the step up to a full time contract at Hearts ahead of this season.

The technically gifted midfielder has clearly made an impression on the Hearts coaching staff, as he was given the nod to join the team on the pre-season tour of Ireland in July 2017. Aged just 16 at the time, Harry displayed a maturity far beyond his years with a series of impressive displays in midfield. Judging by his excellent performances for Hearts U20 in 2016/17, coupled with his promising displays during pre-season, the future looks very bright indeed for Harry.

Chris Hamilton

Chris was another one of the eight young talents to be given a professional contract ahead of the 2017/18 season.

The defender is held in high regards at Riccarton and has also been recognised at international level, having been awarded the Scotland captaincy in last year's Victory Shield.

In addition to the coaching received at the Hearts Academy, the talented youngster has also benefitted from attending Edinburgh's SFA Performance School. Few would bet against him going on to make the grade with the Hearts first team.

THE ARCHIBALI

LEITCH STAND 1914-2017

END OF AN ERA

A 103-year reign came to an end in 2017 as the Archibald Leitch stand was leveled with the ground in order to pave way to a brand new Main Stand at Tynecastle Park.

On Sunday May 7th 2017, Hearts hosted Aberdeen in what would be the last ever game played in front of the old Main Stand. Within a matter of hours of the full-time whistle, work began to strip the interiors of the stand with a view to starting demolition work a few days later.

Everything from door signs and windows to photographs, chairs and bath tubs were carefully removed and placed in storage before being auctioned off a few weeks later. Even the owl statue, used to fend off birds on the roof of the stand, was put up for auction before eventually selling for over £4,000! A total of 147 items were auctioned during a highly successful event in the Gorgie Suite, including six original turnstiles that were each sold for a four-figure sum.

Other auction highlights included several unique wooden signs, bearing messages discouraging nuisance behavior, which sold for over £5,000 over all. In total, close to £70,000 was raised from the auction, a quite incredible sum that speaks volumes for how much the Main Stand meant to Hearts supporters.

By the time the Jambos played their first home pre-season game, against Newcastle United on July 14th, the Archibald Leitch Stand had disappeared from the Gorgie skyline and replaced with the "skeleton" of the new Main Stand. For supporters seated in the Wheatfield Stand, it represented one of the last chances to enjoy a view of Edinburgh Castle before the new stand was filled in.

A total of three games were played at

NOTICE

ANY PERSON COMMITTING A NUISANCE IN THE GROUNDS WILL BE PROSECUTED.

GENTLEMEN

Photo: Ray French

Tynecastle in the summer of 2017, all of which took place in front of just three stands as construction continued on the new Main Stand. Changing rooms and a tunnel were constructed beneath the Wheatfield Stand in order to accommodate home and visiting teams. These facilities will be used for many years to come, primarily by youth teams using the community pitch at the rear of the Wheatfield Stand.

Overall, the summer of 2017 will be remembered as the time when the face of Tynecastle Park change on an almost weekly basis as the new Main Stand neared completion.

The History of the Main Stand

Over the course of its 103-year existence, the Main Stand at Tynecastle Park saw it all: the hoisting of League Championship Trophies; Cup winning celebrations; legendary players; dramatic Edinburgh Derbies and some incredible European nights under the floodlights. There were highs and lows throughout: 1,261 Hearts wins, 507 defeats and 484 draws. The Maroon faithful celebrated 4,687 goals and looked on with anguish at the 2,624 goals conceded. Here is a brief overview of some of the highlights of the Archibald Leitch Stand's 103-year reign.

1913: With complaints about congestion in the existing Main Stand on the rise, Hearts Manager and Club Secretary John McCartney raised the issue of building a new Main Stand. Archibald Leitch was commissioned and the initial cost was estimated at £6,000.

1914: A revised estimate of £8,000 was submitted. Hearts had £4,000 in the bank and raised an additional £2,500 through the sale of Percy Dawson to Blackburn Rovers (a record British fee at the time). A warrant to commence construction was issued on 13th April 1914. The New Stand was partially opened on 15th August that year when Hearts beat Celtic 2-0 in the league before a crowd of 18,000.

1914 – The Grand Opening: Upon completion, the New Stand boasted 4,100 seats with 6,000 standing places under cover. It was the most advanced stand in Scotland, boasting modern toilet facilities, electric lighting, drinking wells, a billiard room and a gymnasium. The final cost had by this point reached £12,780.

1926: As the country recovered from the traumas of The Great War, Hearts experienced an unprecedented demand from supporters. On 20th February 1926, 51,000 packed into Tynecastle for the visit of Celtic in a Scottish Cup third round tie. A further 10,000 were turned away at the gates. Celtic won 4-0.

1948: Following on from the Second World War, Hearts again began to enjoy huge attendances at Tynecastle with fans sensing a special team was being built. On 9th October 1948, Manager David McLean introduced the dazzling attacking trio of Alfie Conn, Willie Bauld and Jimmy Wardhaugh before a crowd of 24,734. East Fife were swept aside that day with Bauld scoring a hat trick in a 6-1 rout. He quickly became known as The King of Hearts.

1954: Tynecastle's capacity reaches 54,359 as it becomes the first ground in Scotland to have all its standing areas made of concrete. In October that year, Hearts beat Motherwell in the Scottish League Cup Final to secure the club's first major trophy in 48 years.

1956: Hearts' Golden era begins as Manager Tommy Walker leads the team to Scottish Cup glory against Celtic in April.

1957-1960: The Jambos' win the League Championship in 1957/58 (scoring a record 132 goals) and 1959/60, as well as the League Cup in 1958 and 1959.

1962: The League Cup is won once again and Hearts enter European football on a regular basis. Hearts now have average home gates above 20,000.

1972: Tynecastle hosts its last ever crowd in excess of 40,000 when 40,354 fan watched a 1-0 defeat to Celtic in the Scottish Cup.

1976: On 29th September, Hearts defeated Lokomotive Leipzig 5-1 in a stunning Cup Winners Cup display before a crowd of 17,247.

1977: 6th April was a dark day in Gorgie as a home defeat to Ayr United condemned Heart of Midlothian to the first relegation in the club's history.

1981: After a rollercoaster period of relegations and falling attendances, Wallace Mercer buys a controlling interest in Hearts. It was the beginning of Hearts' revival.

1982: Alex MacDonald is appointed Manager in February and wins promotion in 1982/83. He is instrumental in turning the club's fortunes around with a team built around the likes of John Colquhoun, Craig Levein, Dave MacPherson, Henry Smith, Sandy Jardine and the one and only John Robertson.

1982-1989: Hearts return to Europe and come agonisingly close to winning the League Title in 85/86. That season saw average home gates of 16,198 – the highest for 25 years. The Jambos also reached the Quarter Finals of the UEFA Cup in 1988/89. A crowd of 26,294 saw Hearts beat Bayern

Munich courtesy of a Iain Ferguson free kick; a goal many believe sparked the most frenzied Tynecastle celebrations of all-time.

1994: Tynecastle undergoes considerable modernisation, including the construction of the Wheatfield Stand. On 12th January, the Main Stand helps play host to the last 20,000 plus crowd at Tynecastle in a 1-1 League Cup Draw against Hibs. 23 years would pass before Tynecastle could again host crowds of over 20,000.

1997: The Gorgie Stand is completed and boasts 3,400 seats.

1998: A 42 year wait for more Scottish Cup glory comes to an end as Jim Jefferies' Hearts bring the Cup back to Gorgie following a 2-1 win over Rangers at Celtic Park. Close to 200,000 fans pack out the streets of Edinburgh to honour the heroes in maroon, culminating in a celebration on the Tynie turf as yet another trophy is hoisted in front of the Main Stand.

2006: A Paul Hartley penalty in May 2006 seals a 1-0 win over Aberdeen and sends Hearts into the Champions League Qualifiers. This comes under the Vladimir Romanov era, a man whose arrival two years prior temporarily halted concerts over the future of Tynecastle Park.

2008: Planning applications to construct a 10,000 capacity Main Stand are submitted but the application eventually stalls. The club's total debt reached £37 million.

2012: The Main Stand again plays host to Scottish Cup celebrations as jubilant Jambos bask in the glory of a 5-1 destruction of city rivals Hibs at Hampden.

2014: Financial problems send the club into administration and the very future of Heart of Midlothian is at risk. The team starts the 2013/14 season with a 15 point deduction and are eventually relegated. In June 2014, the club comes out of administration and into the welcome hands of Ann Budge and the Foundation of Hearts.

2015: The club's remarkable turnaround sees Robbie Neilson's men lift the Championship trophy before a sold-out Tynecastle in May. Hearts' relentless campaign saw them win the title in spectacular fashion, leaving Hibs and Rangers for dust.

2017: On 7th May, the Main Stand takes its final bow as Hearts host Aberdeen. A 103-year era comes to an end as the historic structure makes way for a brand new, modern Main Stand that raises the Tynecastle capacity to over 20,000.

Thanks to Ray French and Ray Scoble for supplying some of the Main Stand images.

Photo by Ray French

The Manager Craig Levein

Having spent the three previous years as the club's Director of Football, the then 52-year-old former Scotland manager was asked by the Board of Directors to return to the Tynecastle dugout for the first time in 13 years.

Craig was brought back to the club in 2014 to assist Ann Budge with rebuilding Hearts in the wake of administration. He was tasked with rebuilding the football department and much of his focus was directed towards the club's academy, which urgently required an overhaul following years of under investment. The Hearts Academy today is in a far better shape, which in turn made it possible forCraig to combine his Director of Football role with managing the first team.

As he was unveiled to the press as manager for a second time, he admitted he was delighted to get back into the dugout.

"I've missed it, no question about that. I've missed the pressure of standing down there, 4-2 down to Hibs in injury time," said Craig at the time.

He was, of course, referring to the dramatic 4-4 match against Hibs in January 2003 when the Jambos scored twice in added on time to seal the unlikeliest of points against their fiercest rivals. It is one of a countless number of memorable moments enjoyed by the Fife-born manager during his first spell in charge.

The former Hearts captain was appointed manager first time round in December 2000 before departing for Leicester City four years later. During that time he secured two consecutive third place finishes in the league, thereby becoming the first Hearts manager to steer the club into back-to-back European campaigns since the 1960s.

He steered Hearts to a fifth place finish in his first half season before repeating the feat the following year. By that time, however, he was well on the way to building a successful side and the next two league campaigns proved highly enjoyable for those of a maroon persuasion.

The Jambos finished third behind the Old Firm in the 2002/03 season, thereby securing a most welcome return to Europe. Their continental adventure began the next season, with a Mark de Vries goal securing a fantastic 1-0 victory away to Bordeaux. A 2-0 defeat at Tynecastle eliminated the Gorgie boys, but Hearts returned for a second bite at the cherry the following season.

On August 28th 2017, Craig Levein was appointed Hearts Manager for a second time.

Portuguese side Braga were knocked out 5-3 on aggregate in the first round of the UEFA Cup, before the group stages saw them pitted against Feyenoord, Schalke 04, Ferencvaros and Basel. The latter produced the most memorable night as an 89th minute Robbie Neilson strike sealed a 2-1 win in Switzerland. By that time, however, Craig had left the club to join Leicester City and a further ten years would pass until he returned.

In addition to Leicester City, he enjoyed spells with Raith Rovers, Dundee United and Scotland before coming home to Tynecastle. A former captain, two-time manager and Director of Football, Craig Levein's relationship with Hearts stretches back over 30 years. Fingers crossed for more European adventures during his second spell in the hot seat!

Don Cowie

FACTFILE:

Don Cowie

Did you know...?

Don Cowie made his debut in English football against Premiership giants Chelsea.

Don played his first game for Scotland against Japan in 2009. He went on to win ten caps.

Don started his career at Ross County, who his dad also played for before they joined the professional leagues.

Don finished as top scorer for Inverness Caledonian Thistle in season 2007/08, when he bagged nine goals.

Don has won two trophies in his career; the Scottish Challenge Cup with Ross County in 2006/07 and the English Championship title with Cardiff City in 2012/13.

Don has played over 500 first-team games in total in a career spanning 17 years to date.

Don scored a penalty in the League Cup Final shootout against Liverpool at Wembley in 2011/12. The match ended 2-2 after extra time, but it was Liverpool who won the trophy after coming out on top in the 3-2 penalty shootout.

Don's first goal for Hearts came against his old team Inverness Caledonian Thistle in August 2016. He grabbed his second Hearts goal later on in the same game.

Don has played against two World Cup winning teams with Scotland. He featured against Brazil in a 2-0 friendly defeat in London in 2011 and later that year came on against Spain in a 3-1 European Championships qualifying defeat in Alicante.

Don has worked under managers such as John Robertson, Malky Mackay, Ole Gunnar Solskjaer and Brendan Rodgers during his career.

Christophe Berra

FACTFILE: Christophe Berra

Did you know...?

Christophe Berra made his debut for Hearts in a 2003 2-1 defeat at Dundee United, aged 18.

His first Hearts goal came in 2005/06 in a 2-0 win over Kilmarnock.

He got a Scottish Cup Winner's medal after being part of the 2012 squad that beat Gretna on penalties in the final at Hampden.

Christophe became the league's youngest captain when he was handed the armband in 2007/08.

Although capped for Scotland, Christophe could've represented France through his dad.

He bagged himself another medal when he helped Wolverhampton Wanderers to the English Championship title in 2008/09.

Christophe scored Scotland's winning goal in a 2015 1-0 victory over Northern Ireland at Hampden. Now-Hearts teammate Aaron Hughes played for Northern Ireland that night, and Kyle Lafferty was on the substitute bench.

Although his appearance in the Betfred Cup defeat to Dunfermline at the start of the season was his fourth since returning to the club, it was the 150th time he has pulled on the famous maroon shirt overall.

Christophe made nearly 350 appearances south of the border for Wolves and Ipswich Town after spending nine years playing in the Premier League and Championship.

He made his Scotland debut against Czech Republic in 2011 and has gone on to win a further 35 caps.

Meet the coaches

Craig Levein
Manager

Austin MacPhee
Assistant Coach

Liam Fox
First Team Coach

Jon Daly
First Team Coach

Paul Gallacher
Goalkeeping Coach

Andy Kirk
U20s Coach

U20 Fixtures and Results 2016/17

League / Cup	Day	Date	Opponent	H/A	Score	Goal scorers
Irn Bru Cup	Tues	Aug 2	**Stirling Albion**	A	3-2	Jones / Roy / Mclean
Irn Bru Cup	Tues	Aug 16	**Elgin City**	A	0-2	
League	Tues	Aug 23	**Hibernian**	A	2-2	Johnsen / Mclean
League	Mon	Aug 29	**Dundee United**	H	1-1	Morrison
League	Tues	Sep 6	**Hamilton**	A	0-1	
League	Mon	Sep 12	**Kilmarnock**	H	0-1	
League	Mon	Sep 19	**St Johnstone**	A	0-0	
League	Wed	Sep 28	**Dunfermline**	A	3-2	Currie 3
League	Mon	Oct 3	**Celtic**	A	1-3	Currie
League	Mon	Oct 10	**Ross County**	H	0-2	
League	Tues	Oct 18	**Partick Thistle**	A	1-3	Irving
Sfa Cup 3	Sun	Oct 23	**Annan Athletic**	H	10-0	Morrison 2 / Currie 2 / Irving / Roy 3 / Leonard / Petkov
League	Mon	Oct 31	**Dundee**	H	2-1	Buaben / Currie
League	Wed	Nov 9	**Motherwell**	A	1-0	Muirhead
League	Mon	Nov 14	**St Mirren**	H	1-2	Ackers (tr)
League	Tues	Nov 22	**Falkirk**	A	1-1	Mcdonald
League	Mon	Nov 28	**Rangers**	H	1-2	Mclean
Sfa Cup 4	Sun	Dec 4	**Rangers**	H	2-5	Hamilton / Henderson
League	Wed	Dec 7	**Inverness Ct**	A	2-2	Morrison / Vladislav
League	Wed	Dec 14	**Aberdeen**	H	0-2	
League	Wed	Dec 21	**Dundee United**	A	2-2	Zanatta / Jones
League	Mon	Jan 16	**Hamilton**	H	3-0	Quitongo (og) / Irving / Currie
League	Tues	Jan 24	**Kilmarnock**	A	0-1	
League	Mon	Jan 30	**St Johnstone**	H	3-0	Henderson 2 / Irving (pen)
League	Mon	Feb 6	**Dunfermline**	H	1-1	Petkov
League	Mon	Feb 13	**Celtic**	H	1-0	Roy
League	Mon	Feb 20	**Ross County**	A	1-4	Irving
League	Tues	Feb 28	**Partick Thistle**	H	5-1	Roy 3 / Irving / Reid
League	Tues	Mar 14	**Dundee**	A	2-1	Morrison / Bikey
League	Mon	Mar 20	**Motherwell**	H	0-3	
League	Tues	Mar 28	**St Mirren**	A	1-2	Roy
League	Mon	Apr 3	**Falkirk**	H	3-1	Roy / Henderson 2
League	Mon	Apr 10	**Rangers**	A	1-2	Moore
League	Mon	Apr 17	**Inverness Ct**	H	3-1	Moore 3
League	Tues	Apr 25	**Aberdeen**	A	3-1	Currie 3
League	Mon	May 1	**Hibernian**	H	3-1	Nicholson / Currie (pen) Roy

SHINING STAR

Kyle Lafferty

9

Position: Striker

Date of Birth: 16 Sept 1987

Place of Birth: Enniskillen, Northern Ireland

- As of August 2017, Kyle had represented Northern Ireland on 59 occasions, scoring 20 goals. He made his debut in May 2006.

- Kyle was his country's topscorer during the Euro 2016 qualifying stages, bagging a total of seven goals.

- His previous spell in Scotland saw him score 36 goals in 134 games for Rangers.

- Kyle scored the only goal of the game in his competitive debut for Hearts, a 1-0 win over Elgin City in the Betfred Cup.

- Kyle's goal against Peterhead in the Betfred Cup saw him become the 14th Hearts player in history to score in every one of his first three competitive games.

- Kyle began his professional career with English club Burnley before joining Rangers in 2008.

- Kyle signed for the Jambos in June 2017 and was given the number 9 jersey.

Kyle Lafferty

Summer Arrivals

Jon McLaughlin
GOALKEEPER

The Edinburgh-born shot-stopper signed for Hearts in August from English side Burton Albion.

He has spent a number of years down south, amassing over 300 appearances for Burton and Bradford City. He won back-to-back promotions with Burton, going from League Two to the Championship.

Ross Callachan
MIDFIELDER

Ross signed from Raith Rovers on a two year deal on Deadline Day in August 2017.

Kyle Lafferty

STRIKER

The 30-year-old striker joined the Jambos as a free agent back in June following the expiration of his contract with Norwich City.

The prolific frontman previously spent four years in Scotland with Rangers between 2008 and 2012 and has since established himself as a key member of the Northern Ireland squad.

He scored on his competitive Hearts debut in a 3-0 win over East Fife and went on to add a further three goals in his next four appearances.

Cole Stockton

STRIKER

The Liverpool-born centre forward arrived in Gorgie on a two-year deal following the expiration of his contract at Tranmere Rovers.

He came through the youth ranks at Tranmere before making his professional debut in 2012. He scored 18 times in his final season before joining Hearts and continued his goalscoring form for the Jambos by netting in his first outing against Livingston in a pre-season friendly.

Michael Smith

DEFENDER

Michael brings a wealth of experience to the Hearts right-back position, having joined from English side Peterborough for a nominal fee. The Northern Ireland cap made over 130 first team appearances for The Posh before signing a two-year deal in Gorgie. His good form for Peterborough saw him earn a Northern Ireland appearance in March 2016 against Slovenia.

Ashley Smith-Brown

DEFENDER

Hearts boosted their defensive options with the capture of left-back Ashley-Smith Brown on season-long loan from English giants Manchester City. The Manchester-born defender is a product of the Man City academy, having joined his hometown club at the age of 10. He spent last season on loan at Dutch side NAC Breda and played a key role in helping them secure promotion back to the top flight.

Rafal Grzelak

DEFENDER

The towering Polish defender spent the previous two seasons playing in Poland's top-flight before signing a two-year deal with Hearts in the summer. Strong in the tackle, Rafal is a versatile player who is equally adept in midfield.

Manuel Milinkovic

MIDFIELDER

The French/ Serbian winger joined on season-long loan from Genoa on Deadline Day in August 2017.

Connor Randall

MIDFIELDER

The 21-year-old versatile midfielder joined Hearts on season-long loan from Liverpool at the end of July.

He made his competitive debut in the league opener at Celtic Park, having spent much of last season playing for Liverpool U23s. He has numerous Liverpool first team games to his name, having appeared for the Reds in the Premier League, FA Cup and League Cup.

Christophe Berra

DEFENDER

The former Hearts captain returned to Tynecastle this summer to reclaim the captain's armband, much to the delight of the club's supporters.

The Scotland international left the Jambos in 2009 and has since played for Wolverhampton Wanderers and Ipswich Town. He penned a three-year deal with Hearts and returns to Gorgie with a wealth of experience under his belt.

Answers

Quiz p30

1. Christophe Berra
2. Arnaud Djoum
3. Nou Camp
4. 103 years old
5. John Robertson
6. Tynecastle Park
7. Elgin City
8. Northern Ireland
9. St Mirren
10. Rangers

Beat the Goalie p34

1. John Robertson
2. 1874
3. Paulo Sergio
4. St Mirren
5. Alan Shearer
6. Portsmouth
7. Madrid
8. Man Utd
9. Celtic and Aberdeen
10. 10
11. Ajax
12. False
13. Stoke City
14. Madrid
15. Yellow
16. Seaweed
17. Canadian
18. Sir Bobby Robson
    Roy Hodgson
    Kevin Keegan

Hearts Wordsearch p32

J	M	D	**G**	D	Q	W	T	**H**	H	D	K
N	F	C	F	O	N	Y	U	V	H	F	H
N	O	G	P	P	N	G	G	W	R	W	G
O	R	O	K	H	H	C	Y	N	X	C	E
T	G	T	R	E	R	Z	A	T	P	I	H
K	**G**	M	S	A	M	C	M	L	W	Q	D
C	O	V	N	L	**M**	B	Z	O	V	P	W
O	R	A	C	R	M	Q	**C**	W	R	E	Z
T	G	R	F	Q	T	B	B	R	Z	Q	S
S	I	R	**E**	D	I	N	B	U	R	G	H
W	E	E	L	T	S	A	C	E	N	Y	**T**
W	N	**B**	J	Y	T	R	E	F	F	A	**L**

Hearts Crossword p32

		A						J						
A	R	N	A	U	D	D	J	O	U	R	N			
A		N						C						
R		B			C			K						
O		U			R			T						
N		D			A			H						
H		G			I			E						
U		E			G			J						
G			K	Y	L	E	L	A	F	F	E	R	T	Y
H					E			M						
E					V			B						
S					E			O						
					I									
		J	O	H	N	R	O	B	E	R	T	S	O	N

Spot the Difference p33

Where's Jock?

Jock the Jambo is always keen to lend a helping hand. Over the course of the summer, he was busy helping with the construction of the new Main Stand.
Can you spot him in this photo?